Do
You
Believe?

RICKY CLEMONS

PUBLISHED BY FIDELI PUBLISHING, INC.

ISBN: 978-1-962402-62-0

Published by

Fideli Publishing, Inc.
119 W. Morgan St.
Martinsville, IN 46151
www.FideliPublishing.com

Table of Contents

Do You Believe?

Do you believe your thoughts?

Do you believe your words?

Do you believe your actions?

Do you believe your dreams?

Do you believe your appetite?

Do you believe your feelings?

Do you believe you?

Do you believe your eyes?

Do you believe your talents?

Do you believe your spiritual gifts?

Do you believe the bible?

Do you believe in Jesus Christ?

Do you believe truth?

Do you know what to believe?

Do you believe what you sing?

Do you believe what you read?

Believing is very powerful.

Believing is very real.

Believing is very effective, whether you believe you are right or wrong.

Believing in Jesus Christ is an eternal belief that will surely guarantee you and me to one day enter into heaven with Jesus when he comes back again.

Do you believe your ears?

Do you believe your nose?

Do you believe your body?

Believing can be an abundance of life in Jesus Christ.

Believing can be a short life for believing the devil's lies.

Believing is the key to lock the door of your destiny, because believing is the reason for the choice that you make.

Believing is the strong backbone of every choice that you make.

Do you believe your heart?

Do you believe your life?

Do you believe your health?

Do you believe your tradition?

Lucifer had believed that he could take God's place on God's holy throne, causing him to rebel against God.

You and me can believe a lot of things, and every day we believe to live if we are not ill in our mind to kill oneself.

You and me will believe something before we ever make a choice.

The choice that we make will surely affirm what you and me believe.

Do you believe that you exist to love and obey Jesus Christ?

Do you believe that you will become like who you believe in?

Do you believe that Jesus is above whoever and whatever you believe?

If you and me believe in Jesus Christ, we will be like Jesus Christ in our daily living.

If you and me believe the devil, we will be like the devil.

Do you believe that your choices in life are the results of what you believe in from day to day?

Believing is before any action that is seen because what you and me believe, we will do, whether it's good or bad.

If you believe that you must eat food to live, you will eat food to live.

If you believe that you must drink water to live, you will drink water to live.

Believing is what God has given to you and me to use for our good of believing in His Son Jesus Christ who the demons believe with fear and tremble whenever you and I call on the name of the Lord Jesus Christ.

Do you believe what is right and what is wrong that you will choose to think, say and do from the results of whoever you believe and whatever you believe from day to day.

Do you believe your knowledge?

Do you believe your intelligence?

Do you believe your common sense?

Do you believe that God gave you the freedom to believe whatever that you want to believe?

Do you believe that a robot will do something different from what you programmed it to do?

God didn't create you and me to be a robot that can't believe anyone or anything but will only do what you program it to do.

Do you believe that Jesus Christ is the son of God and the life eternal?

Do you believe that Jesus gave up his life on the cross for your sins?

Do you believe that Jesus got the victory over death and the grave?

Do you believe that if you believe in Jesus Christ he will save you from your sins?

God gave you and me the freedom to live by who we believe and what we believe.

Who we believe and what we believe can never ascent above God the Father, God the Son and God the Holy Spirit who is the origin of the bible that you and me can always believe and live by with no regrets to denounce the highest belief that is rooted and grounded in Jesus Christ.

Do you believe your trials?

Do you believe your ups and downs in life?

Do you believe your comings and goings?

Do you believe your testimonies?

Do you believe your education?

Do you believe your mistakes?

Do you believe your motives?

Do you believe your intentions?

Do you believe your purpose?

Do you believe your choices that are the results of your beliefs day after day.

Do you believe that Jesus Christ is your only salvation?

Do you believe that Jesus Christ is your only living hope?

Do you believe that Jesus Christ is your only undying love?

Do you believe that Jesus Christ is who you can always trust to love you, even if you don't love him?

Do you believe that Jesus Christ is your best friend?

Do you believe that Jesus Christ will never leave you or forsake you?

Do you believe that Jesus Christ won't give up on you, even if you give up on yourself?

Believing is in its highest and greatest place of existence in this world, if we believe in Jesus Christ who has overcome every false belief in this world.

Believing in anyone else or anything else more than believing in Jesus will be an eternal regret for us to miss out on heaven where angels believe in Jesus Christ to be the son of God and the creator of all things.

Do you believe your theories?

Do you believe your plans?

Do you believe your pretense?

Do you believe your hypothesis?

Do you believe your opinions?

Do you believe your prejudice?

Do you believe your freedom?

Do you believe your bondage?

Do you believe your love?

Do you believe your hatred?

Do you believe your difference?

Do you believe your fear?

Do you believe your courage?

Do you believe your existence in life?

Do you believe your victories?

Do you believe your defeats?

Do you believe what you have been through in your life?

Do you believe what you are going through in your life?

Do you believe your wealth?

Do you believe your poverty?

Do you believe your blessings?

Do you believe your curse?

Do you believe your destiny?

If you and I believe in ourselves or anyone else and anything else more than we believe in Jesus Christ, we are doomed to be like the wind that blows in different directions, for only Jesus to always know where we will blow to in our wayward beliefs.

Believing can be a hurricane down in the soul.

Believing can be an earthquake down in the soul.

Believing can be a wildfire down in the soul.

Believing can be a tornado down in the soul.

Believing can be a volcano to erupt down in the soul.

Believing can be a flood down in the soul.

Believing can be a train wreck down in the soul.

Believing can be a tidal wave down in the soul.

Believing can be a piled-up car wreck down in the soul.

Believing can surely be a bad thing if you and me don't believe in Jesus Christ who is the fulfillment of the bible that we can always believe to be the truth about Jesus who the devil and his fallen angels believe to come back again on the clouds of glory.

The devil believes that he can run throughout the earth to devourer whoever that he can to cause them to be lost in their sins and miss out on heaven.

Do you believe that you can get your life right with Jesus before it's too late?

Believing is the sunshine down in your soul for believing in Jesus Christ.

Believing is a peaceful river down in your soul for believing is Jesus Christ.

Believing is joy down in your soul for believing in Jesus Christ.

Believing is paradise down in your soul for believing in Jesus Christ.

Believing is a lily in the valley down in your soul for believing in Jesus Christ.

Believing is a beautiful red rose down in your soul for believing in Jesus Christ.

Believing is a beautiful garden down in your soul for believing in Jesus Christ.

Believing is a high mountain down in your soul for believing in Jesus Christ.

Believing is a treasure chest down in your soul for believing in Jesus Christ.

Believing is a gold mine down in your soul for believing in Jesus Christ.

Believing is great wealth down in your soul for believing in Jesus Christ.

Believing is beauty down in your soul for believing in Jesus Christ.

Believing is eternal life down in your soul for believing in Jesus Christ.

Believing is every good thing down in your soul for believing in Jesus Christ.

You and I can believe in Jesus Christ like it's our last day to live, that can't over-shadow our belief that will be sealed in Jesus in the grave, that Jesus will open up and raise us up in His eternal life for believing in Him.

Death and the grave believe that Jesus has all the power to raise the righteous dead when He comes back again on the clouds of glory.

Do you and I believe in Jesus Christ even more than believing that we can die anytime in the day and night that can't stop Jesus from sealing us in His eternal life if we are saved in Him.

If you believe Jesus Christ, your belief is holy.

If you believe in Jesus Christ, your belief is perfect.

Believing in Jesus Christ will get rid of every unbelief in you and me.

Do you believe that Jesus always knows what is good and best for you?

Do you believe to serve your master, whether it be money, material things, a human being or Jesus Christ?

Do you believe a surprise that is at its best in Jesus Christ who can surprise you and me better than anyone in the world?

Do you believe in luck that has no spiritual things to give to you that only Jesus can do?

Do you believe magic that has no heaven to put you in that only Jesus can do when he comes back again?

Do you believe lies that have no truth that is Jesus Christ who sets you and me free from believing lies?

Do you believe the Church that the devil can go to but Jesus Christ is the head of the church to separate the wheat from the tares, when you and me can pull up a wheat that we may believe to be a tare?

Do you believe your ministry in the church to win souls to Jesus Christ who is the only one who can judge your ministry to be about praising him or praising oneself to want to make oneself look good before others?

Do you believe your beauty that will fade away as you age old?

Believing in Jesus Christ is inner beauty that will not fade away as you age old.

Do you believe in your physical strength that will deteriorate as you age old?

Believing in Jesus Christ is inner strength that will not deteriorate as you age old.

Do you believe your mind that can change at any time?

Believing in Jesus Christ is not judging anyone who Jesus always completely knows to repent or not repent of all of one's sins.

Someone in the church can hold onto a sin for only Jesus to know and judge that someone for having a heart of unbelief in Him.

Holding onto even one unconfessed and unrepentant sin will cause you and me to not believe in Jesus who gave up His life on the cross to save us from all of our sins for us to have no excuse to hold onto even one sin that breaks God's Commandments that are holy, righteous and perfect to show unbelievers that we believe in Jesus Christ.

Do you believe your job that can overwork you and underpay you?

Do you believe your business that can go out of business?

Do you believe your clothes that can fade?

Do you believe your shoes that can wear out?

Do you believe your car that can break down?

Do you believe your government that can shut down?

Do you believe your nation that can go to war?

Do you believe your house that can need repair work?

Do you believe your pets that can give you a big veterinarian bill?

Do you believe your phone that can be corrupted with scammers?

Do you believe your computer that can get a computer virus?

Do you believe social media that can turn against you, if you say something wrong?

Do you believe fame that can turn against you, if you do something wrong?

Do you believe that the bank can protect your money from wire fraud?

Believing in Jesus Christ is surely being wise about what's going on in this world.

Believing in Jesus Christ is spiritual protection being our best protection from the wiles of the devil and his demons and his human agents who is all about causing you and me to not believe in Jesus Christ.

Do you believe your spiritual seeds will grow up into a beautiful spiritual fruit tree on God's holy ground where the Holy Spirit plants your spiritual gifts for you to harvest the field of the world to win souls to Jesus Christ?

Everybody Wants to be Believed

Everybody wants people to believe what they say.

Everybody wants people to believe what they do.

Everybody wants to be believed.

Everybody wants people to believe their ideas.

Everybody wants people to believe their life.

Everybody wants to be believed, whether they tell the truth or lies.

Even a little child wants to be believed.

Everybody wants people to believe their opinions.

Everybody wants to believe themselves.

Everybody wants to believe their eyes.

Everybody wants to believe their feelings.

Everybody wants to believe their senses.

Everybody wants to believe their intelligence.

Everybody wants to be believed.

Everybody wants to believe their taste buds.

Everybody wants to believe their hearts.

Everybody wants to believe their minds.

Everybody wants to be believed, whether they are good or evil.

Anyone not in their right mind wants to believe that they say and do things right.

Even a fool wants to believe they are right.

Everybody wants to be believed, but only Jesus always knows the height and depth of what everyone believes from day to day.

Everybody wants to be believed, but it can't reach up any higher than God's holy word that is eternal belief about Jesus Christ.

The devil wants to be believed day after day to cause many people to tell his lies, because the devil is forever lost in his sins against God.

Most of all, Jesus wants to be believed, and we should believe Him to be the Son of God and our Lord and Savior.

Everybody wants to be believed, but nobody can rise above Jesus who the demons fear and tremble from, because Jesus and His angels cast them out of heaven.

Everybody wants to be believed, and there are people who are so much more believable than you and me.

They can get a lot of things done because they are more believable than you and me.

Everybody wants to be believed, but nobody can out-do all the good things that Jesus did when He lived here on earth without sin.

Everybody wants to be believed, but the cross was much more believable even to the demons who saw Jesus being nailed to it and die on it in the place of every sinner from the beginning of time on earth to the last days.

Everybody wants what they say and do to be believed, but nobody can be more believable than Jesus Christ who rose from the grave with victory over death for our lives to be believed today.

The grave is not more believable than Jesus, who is coming back again on the clouds of glory to raise the righteous from death and change the righteous living from mortal to immortal.

Everybody wants to be believed, but who knows our hearts better than Jesus, who we can believe with all of our hearts?

Our hearts can't be more believable than Jesus.

Our works can't be more believable than Jesus.

Our lives can't be more believable than Jesus.

Everybody wants to be believed, even when time is not on our side and we can die today with not enough believable faith in Jesus to be saved.

Everybody wants to be believed; people who invent things want to be believed.

Everybody wants to be believed; people who write and publish books want to be believed, whether their books are fiction or non-fiction.

Everybody wants to be believed; people who solve a mystery want to be believed.

Everybody wants to be believed; people who are sick and get well want to be believed that they are well.

Everybody wants to be believed; people who make a new discovery want to be believed.

Everybody wants to be believed; people who survive a life-threatening situation want to be believed.

Everybody wants to be believed in one way or another.

Everybody wants to be believed, whether they are a Christian or an atheist.

What is forevermore believable than everybody in this world is Jesus Christ who is the truth, the way and the life of all existence in heaven and on earth.

Everybody wants to be believed, but everybody will not have enough evidence to prove themselves to be believable, especially in the courtroom.

Everybody wants to be believed, but only Jesus Christ is always believable and the demons know that better than everybody in this world.

The demons will fear and tremble because they believed too late that Jesus is forevermore powerful than they are.

Everybody wants to be believed, but nobody can ever be more believable than Jesus Christ, who cast the devil and his angels out of heaven so long before any human being existed.

Lucifer wanted to be believed and thought that he could be God, but he deceived himself and one-third of the angels in heaven.

Everybody wants to be believed, but if anyone believes they are more believable than Jesus Christ, then all the darkness of sin will over-shadow their soul and it will be lost.

Everybody wants to be believed about something, but only Jesus will always have proof of everything that He has done and is doing today.

Everybody wants to be believed, but everybody can't prove themselves believable for saying one thing and doing another thing.

Everybody wants to be believed, but everybody will fall short of the glory of God, even if they mean good and well.

Only Jesus Christ is worthy to always be believed in His holy word.

Jesus is the foundation for anyone to stand on and know that He is always believable in a world of so much disbelief about Jesus Christ, even in many churches.

Everybody wants to be believed in the church, but everybody doesn't love everybody in the church so they are not like Jesus, who loves everybody in and out of the church.

Everybody wants to be believed, but everybody's body language will be observed saying much more than words can say.

Everybody wants to be believed; people who are full of themselves want to be believed.

Everybody wants to be believed and it will sooner or later prove to be good or bad in their lives, showing that the truth is always believable over every lie and that the truth will sooner or later prevail.

Everybody wants to be believed, whether they are telling the truth or telling lies.

Jesus Christ is the only living eternal truth to forever be believed over lies that will one day pass away and not be believable to all the holy saints going with Jesus back to heaven when Jesus comes back again.

Everybody wants to be believed regardless of their personality.

Everybody wants to be believed regardless of their gender.

Everybody wants to be believed regardless of their skin color.

Everybody wants to be believed regardless of their religion.

Everybody wants to be believed regardless of their education.

Everybody wants to be believed regardless of their mental health and physical health.

Everybody wants to be believed by what they say, whether it's the truth or a lie.

Everybody wants to be believed by what they do, whether they have good motives or bad motives.

Everybody wants to be believed, whether they are living free in society or in prison.

Everybody wants to be believed, whether they are free or a slave.

Everybody wants to be believed, whether they are rich or poor.

Everybody wants to be believed, whether they are sane or insane.

Nobody can ever be more believable than Jesus Christ, who the Holy Spirit speaks the truth about in the bible that only a fool would not believe.

Everybody wants to be believed, but not everybody will believe in Jesus Christ who is forevermore believable to all the angels in heaven and forevermore believable to all the unfallen worlds.

Everybody wants to be believed and everybody has that in common.

We all relate to one another that we want to be believed for the rest of our lives.

Everybody wants to be believed, whether they are ignorant, foolish or just down right wicked, but only the Lord Jesus Christ is always worthy to be believable.

Jesus is believable in His holy word and in the lives of devout Christians because many people have repented of their sins and turned to Jesus even way back in the bible days and up to this day.

Everybody wants to be believed, but everybody won't believe Jesus Christ, who is the highest believable supernatural being who gave up His life on the cross to save everybody from their sins.

Jesus rose from the grave to conquer death that wants to be believed by sinners.

God Created us to Socialize

God created us to socialize, and it's mostly women who love to talk.

It's mostly women who can talk to one another with ease.

A lot of women don't have to think about what they will talk about, they just do it with ease.

A lot of us men don't know how to socialize well with one another like women who can talk from sun up to sun down like breathing air in and out of our nostrils.

It's mostly women who have the gift to talk just about anything that they have no problem to talk about on any day.

When I go to church, my church sisters love to socialize and they are so good with doing that, but I have to search for words to say.

The average mother can talk a lot to her children with ease, when the average father will run out of words to say to his children.

A lot of children know that especially their mothers will have a lot of words to say to them when they get into some trouble.

Mostly women and girls are the real talkers every day in the home, on the job, in the church and in this world.

There are men who can talk a lot, but many women will out-number the men when it comes to socializing.

Most of us men can't keep up with the women in talking because the average woman has a mouth that is full of words, even when doing other things while talking.

A lot of us men have a long way to go when it comes to socializing with one another and with women, it's mostly women who can talk all day long and not get tired of talking even to their energetic children who can wear a lot of men down and cause them to run out of words to say.

Jesus' mother must have talked to Jesus more than His earthly father, Joseph.

It's mostly women who will raise up their children with a lot of words to say to them that they will cherish or not cherish for life.

Jesus must have cherished his mother Mary's every word.

The average man cannot out-talk the average woman because God has truly given women the gift to socialize and be the best communicators in this world.

God created us to socialize, but it's mostly women and girls who will usually talk the most every day.

Jesus loves everybody but Jesus probably listens to the prayers of mostly women, more so than the prayers of men.

I believe that women will talk to Jesus more than us men.

Most of us men don't talk to one another.

It's mostly the women who motivate us men to open up and talk about what is on our minds.

When it comes to speaking, most women are better talkers than we men, but the Lord Jesus Christ loves to talk to every man, woman, boy and girl every day that we can listen to Jesus talking to us in love in His holy word.

The Lord also uses many women to get a lot of good things done in this world, where without the socializing of women, most of us men would be at a loss for words to say every day.

As many people do say that behind a great man is a great woman.

I believe that a great woman is the real socializer in the home where her words are more than a few for her husband and children to hear.

God created us to socialize with one another, but mostly women and girls don't easily run out of words to say because talking is one of the greatest gifts from God.

Many People Will Say

Many people will say that you are supposed to love others and accept them for who they are.

The Lord says to love our neighbors, and our neighbors are everybody in this world.

When it comes to accepting people for who they are, does it depend on what kind of acceptance that it is?

Are you and I supposed to accept people for being a liar?

Are you and I supposed to accept people for being a fornicator?

By you and me being a Christian, are we supposed to accept people for being an adulterer?

Are you and I supposed to accept people for being a murderer?

Are you and I supposed to accept people for being a manipulator?

By you and me being a Christian, are we supposed to accept people for being a fraud?

Many people will say that you are supposed to love people and accept them for who they are.

Loving others is always the right thing to do by the Lord, who didn't accept the Pharisees for who they were as hypocrites.

Are you and I supposed to accept people for being wicked?

We Christians are supposed to love every person's soul to be saved in Jesus Christ, but we aren't supposed to accept their wicked lifestyles that are not like Jesus.

That word "accept" sounds so good, but if you and I are Christians then we can't accept the wickedness of sin that breaks God's Commandments.

Who in their right mind would accept the devil for who he is?

All sin is from the devil and no true child of God will accept sin.

When Jesus lived in this world, Jesus loved everybody, but He didn't accept people for who they were when they were living in their sins.

Jesus was strongly against that even before He came to this world to save us from our sins.

Many people will say that you are supposed to love everybody, and that is true by God.

When it comes to accepting people for who they are, it depends on what kind of acceptance.

The Lord will not accept you and me for who we are if we are living in our sins, because God hates sin.

He loves our souls and will accept us for being saved in His son Jesus Christ.

If God doesn't accept people for who they are in their wrongdoings, then who are you and I to accept people for who they are in their waywardness?

If you and I are Christians, we truly know that we are supposed to love everybody to be saved in Jesus Christ.

If you and I love Jesus and keep His Commandments, are we supposed to accept people for being a homosexual?

God created a woman for a man, not a man for a man and not a woman for a woman.

God loves everybody, but God won't accept any person's sins.

God didn't accept homosexuality and He destroyed Sodom and Gomorrah.

God loves everybody, but God will never accept people's wickedness, because that is unlike Him.

Many people will say that you are supposed to love everybody and accept them for who they are, but accepting the evil things people do is not right in the eyes of God who won't accept any wickedness in heaven.

Many people will say that we are supposed to love everybody and accept people for who they are.

Are we supposed to accept people for being a serial killer?

Are we supposed to accept people for wanting to rob us or kill us?

God gives us common sense to know that these things are not acceptable.

God commands us to love everybody who is our neighbor, but there are no exceptions to love the evilness of sin in anybody.

We can love everybody, but we can't accept everybody for who they are if they are not living right by God.

God loves every sinner, but God will not accept the acts of their sins.

Your sins will find you and make you who you are if you are not being like Jesus.

Your love and obedience unto Jesus will reveal that you are the Christian that the devil won't accept.

Even the devil has his standards to not accept God for who he is and not accept us Christians for wanting to be like Jesus.

Many people will say that we are supposed to love everybody and accept people for who they are, but the devil doesn't love anyone and won't accept anyone for being a human being who God created in His image and gave us all His grace that the devil will never get from God.

Power Can Corrupt Anyone

Power can corrupt anyone who wants to be in power over other people.

There are political leaders in the government who love to be in power over the people in their nation.

Power can corrupt anyone to commit evil acts to be in power.

Being in power will cause an evil person to feel so proud.

Being in power will cause an evil person to suppress poor people.

Being in power will cause an evil person to bring injustice upon the innocent.

A good person being in power can surely make people's lives much better.

A good person being in power can surely make good things happen.

A good person being in power can surely lighten people's heavy burdens.

A good person being in power can surely change people's lives for the better.

A good person being in power can surely benefit a whole nation.

A good person being in power can surely improve many poor neighborhood areas.

A good person being in power can surely give good people a peace of mind.

Power can corrupt anyone who will use their power for evil.

Lucifer wanted to be in power over God in heaven.

God is all-powerful and Lucifer found out the hard way and was cast out of heaven.

God gave Adam and Eve power over all the earth before they disobeyed Him.

Adam and Eve gave up their power to the devil after they ate that forbidden fruit.

Jesus came to this world and overpowered the devil when Jesus gave up His life on the cross for our sins and rose from the grave with power over death and the grave, giving us eternal life for being saved in Him.

Some of Jesus' disciples wanted Jesus to use His power to rule over the Roman government, but Jesus didn't do that because His mission was all about saving souls from being lost in sin.

Power can corrupt anyone who lives their life to control other people's lives.

God is all-powerful and uses His power in every good way because God doesn't use His power to control anyone —God gave us a free will to choose to love Him or not love Him.

No matter how powerful someone may be, his or her power cannot rise above God who can bring down anyone in power like He brought down King Nebuchadnezzar as well as other kings who believed they were more powerful than God and truly deceived themselves.

God the father, God the Son Jesus Christ and God the Holy Spirit are all-powerful over all the angels, other worlds and every creature on Earth.

The power that God allows anyone to have is only temporary and is to be used to glorify Jesus' holy name.

Power can corrupt anyone for using his or her power to destroy people's lives, and God will get vengeance for this and bring down corrupt people in power so that they know they are not invincible.

Power can corrupt anyone to be hung up on power.

Lucifer was hung up on power and it drove him mad.

Today, the devil would love to have power over everyone in this world.

You and I can thank Jesus for putting a limit on the devil, his demons and his human agents' power so that they can't over-power you and me and make us choose not to love Jesus and keep His Commandments which are freedom from corrupt power.

Power can corrupt anyone, which is like the sun never shining in this world, making it black and dark twenty-four hours around the clock.

Who in their right mind would want to live in a world like that?

Power can surely corrupt anyone to have no shining light from God in them, and make them to be like the dark ocean floor where the sun can't shine down into because of being too deep below the ocean water's surface.

No matter how much power can corrupt anyone who loves to be in power, Jesus has already got the victory over all the world's power and it will be destroyed by His glorious light shining through all the saints when He comes back again on the clouds of glory where every eye shall see Jesus in His eternal power to raise the righteous dead.

The righteous living will see His power and the wicked living will see Jesus' power and drop dead at the brightness of His light that will expose anyone who is greedy for power and they will surely drop dead in the brightness of Jesus' light when He comes back again.

Can Every Action be True?

Can every action be true when there are people who will do something good for the wrong reason?

Can every action be true when there are people who will help someone in need to make themselves look good?

Can every action be true when there are people who will give their children whatever they want and don't need?

If you see someone do something good, does it mean that he or she is good?

There are people who will give you and me something good and want something back in return.

An action can look good with pretense motives.

Can every action be true when an action can deceive you and me to believe that what we see someone do must be for the right reason when it may not be for the right reason?

The reason why there are wolves in sheep's clothing is because their actions will only pretend to be good to deceive people.

The scribes and Pharisees actions were full of pretense as they prayed in public before people to make them believe that they were so holy and righteous.

Jesus called them hypocrites because Jesus saw right through their pretense actions looking good in the public eye but not to Jesus who they couldn't fool.

Can every action be true for you and me to truly know someone who can do something that we believe to be good while they have a hidden agenda to trap us in deceit?

Can every action be true when a serial killer can do something good to convince his victim to go with him to meet their death?

The Devil Especially Hates

The devil especially hates rich Christians because he knows that they will help those who are poor.

The devil especially hates rich Christians because he knows that they have the money to finance the spreading of the gospel of Jesus Christ all around the world.

The devil especially hates rich Christians because he knows that they will make a great spiritual investment to give out bibles and other religious materials to the poor.

The devil especially hates rich Christians because he knows that they will do a lot of good things to uplift the Lord's holy name.

The devil especially hates rich Christians because he knows that they are very powerful witnesses of Jesus Christ to all the world.

The devil especially hates rich Christians because he knows that they will have a great influence over the poor by showing that they love Jesus.

The devil especially hates rich Christians because he knows that they will reach out to so many lost souls asking them to repent and turn to Jesus.

The devil especially hates rich Christians because he knows that they will humble themselves before the Lord Jesus Christ for all the world to see that they don't let their riches puff them up with pride.

The devil especially hates rich Christians because he knows that they will give it all up for Jesus' name sake to amaze the rich worldly people and the poor worldly people to see that they are true to Jesus who gave up all of His riches in heaven to be a poor sinless man to save us from our sins.

The devil especially hates rich Christians because he knows that their testimonies about where Jesus brought them from would change many people's lives to live for Jesus Christ.

The devil especially hates rich Christians because he knows that they will go above and beyond themselves to help the poor and look for nothing back in return except hoping that people will believe in Jesus Christ to be saved before it is too late.

The devil hated Abraham who was rich.

The devil hated Job who was rich.

The devil hated King Solomon who was rich.

Their riches were from the Lord to glorify His holy name, especially in the presence of the poor who Jesus said would always be around.

Telling People the Truth is Not Judging Them

Many people will say that you are judging them if you tell them the truth about what they are doing wrong.

Telling people the truth about themselves is not judging them, it's simply stating the fact that what they are doing is wrong.

Many people will use the word "judging" in the wrong way, to avoid the truth about what they are doing wrong.

Judging people is saying that they will never change and do what is right.

Judging people is saying that they know better when they may not know better to do what is right.

Judging people is saying that they will never be any good.

Judging people is saying that they are hopeless.

Judging people is saying that they are going to hell.

Only the Lord knows the heart completely, and His judgement is only fair.

Only the Lord knows who will go with Him to heaven when He comes back again.

Only the Lord knows His true righteous children who are saved in Him.

Telling people about what they are doing wrong is not judging them.

Telling them the truth is letting them know that you know what they are doing is wrong, even if they don't know it and may believe that you are judging them.

Jesus is the truth to set everybody free from the devil's lies, but Jesus will judge everybody's hearts whether they have good motives or bad motives.

Only Jesus knows everybody's motives and intentions to be true or false, and Jesus will judge them.

You and I don't know every motive and intention in people's hearts to judge them, but we can tell them the truth in love about what they say being wrong or what they do being wrong and we can do this by knowing the truth of God's holy word.

Judging someone is saying that he or she are a lost case, when Jesus can save the worst sinner, like Jesus saved the demon possessed man who had a legion of demons in him.

Jesus cast those demons out of him and made him sane so he could go back to his hometown to tell the people that Jesus healed him.

The man told people the truth, even though some of them probably judged him and Jesus to be deceptive.

A Spiritual War

We are in a spiritual war of different religious beliefs fighting against each other day after day.

This spiritual war has been going on for thousands of years, but in these last days the spiritual war is much worse.

In this spiritual war, the Muslim beliefs are fighting the Christian beliefs every day.

The Judaism beliefs are fighting the Christian beliefs every day.

The Hindu beliefs are fighting the Christian beliefs every day.

The Buddhism beliefs are fighting the Christian beliefs every day.

The Christian beliefs are attacked the most by other religious beliefs because the Christian beliefs are all about believing in Jesus Christ.

All the other religious beliefs don't believe that Jesus is the Son of God.

All the other religious beliefs claim to worship God, but will not acknowledge that Jesus Christ is the Son of God.

We are in a spiritual war for believing in Jesus Christ, who other religious beliefs will deny to be the Son of God.

The Christian belief is the one and only right belief that will surely win this spiritual war when Jesus comes back again on the clouds of glory.

This spiritual war goes on every day all around the world where the Christian beliefs are demonized the most for believing in Jesus Christ.

We are in a spiritual war because many religious beliefs believe that there is a God to worship, but will denounce Jesus Christ, claiming He was only a prophet and not the Son of God.

This spiritual war has caused many physical wars since back in the bible days when rebellious people rejected the prophets of God and didn't believe the prophetic messages.

We are in a spiritual war that goes way back to Genesis 3:15 that says, "I will put enmity between thee and the woman, and thy seed and her seed: he shall crush thy head, and thou shalt bruise his heel".

There Are People Who

There are people who see wrong in everybody else except themselves.

There are people who love knowledge but will only use it for evil.

There are people who mean well to speak the truth but can be ignorant to some true facts.

There are people who believe that they have good mental health, but they are full of hate.

There are people who have never been out of their country, but they act like they have been around the world.

There are people who have never had a drink of alcohol, but their ways are changable, like someone who is drunk.

There are religious people whose words are as smooth as oil, but their actions are like the wind blowing in different directions.

There are church folks who are very good at quoting bible scriptures, but they don't love everybody.

There are church folks who are silent about giving testimonies of what Jesus brought them through, but they are very expressive about how good they are doing in their lives today.

There are people who will put us believers in Jesus Christ under their microscope of opinion and call us delusional, but when they are on their death beds they hope that our prayers will be heard for Jesus to heal them.

The Lord Can Use Anybody

The Lord can use anybody to help you and me regardless of the color of their skin.

There are good men and women who don't go to church at all, but the Lord can use them to help you and me in some kind of way.

It doesn't matter what age people are, the Lord can use them to help you and me.

We just don't know when we will need someone to help us.

The Lord can use anybody to help you and me in some kind of way.

One day, I went to the gas pump to put some gas in my car and when I had finished pumping my gas, I got back in my car and drove down the road.

It was raining that day, and someone drove up a little ways to pass me in the left lane.

I saw a man with his head out of the passenger side window.

He was trying to get my attention by pointing his finger at my car.

I didn't notice what he was trying to tell me until I looked in my side view mirror on my car and saw that I had forgotten to screw my gas cap back on my car gas tank.

I know that the Lord used that man to try to get my attention so I would look and see what he was pointing at on that rainy day.

If the Lord had not used that man to get my attention, I would have kept on driving my car with my gas tank open for the rain water to get in my gas tank and maybe cause some problems in my gas tank.

The Lord can use anybody to help you and me at anytime, anywhere.

No matter what race, creed or culture, the Lord can use anybody for his purpose.

No Christian is Exempted From

No Christian is exempted from going through some trials for Jesus' name sake.

Every Christian will go through a hardship for Jesus' name sake.

The Christian journey is not an easy street to walk down.

No Christian is exempted from grieving over a loved one.

No Christian is exempted from feeling pain.

No Christian is exempted from being disappointed.

No Christian is exempted from being discouraged.

No Christian is exempted from being falsely accused.

No Christian is exempted from being jealous of.

No Christian is exempted from being disrespected.

No Christian is exempted from being talked bad about.

No Christian is exempted from being treated badly.

No Christian is exempted from being put down.

No Christian is exempted from being misunderstood.

No Christian is exempted from being called a hypocrite.

No Christian is exempted from being called a liar.

No Christian is exempted from being accused of playing church.

No Christian is exempted from going through trials for Jesus' name sake.

No Christian is exempted from being tempted by the devil.

No Christian is exempted from getting sick.

No Christian is exempted from going through hardships for Jesus' name sake.

Jesus will be in the trials with you and me to give us the strength to endure the trials that Jesus won't allow to always last.

Our trials make us more like Jesus who went through hardships and died on the cross to save us from our sins.

Our hardships don't come close to the hardships that Jesus went through to save all sinners.

Our trials are only for a moment compared to the eternal easy life that Jesus will give to every Christian when He comes back again to take us to heaven.

The Bible Truth

The things that go on in this world are from the truth of the bible prophecy that God's prophets predicted would happen.

The bible truth is what goes on in this world every day that philosophies, theories, educated guesses, science, opinions, phenomenon, spiritualism, luck, magic, wishes and lies cannot rise above.

The bible truth is the real deal about everything that is going on in this world where philosophies are so artificial compared to the bible truth.

The bible truth is the real deal about everything that is going on in this world where theories are so artificial compared to the bible truth.

The bible truth is the real deal about everything that is going on in this world where educated guesses are so artificial compared to the bible truth.

The bible truth is the real deal about everything that is going on in this world where science is so artificial compared to the bible truth.

The bible truth is the real deal about everything that is going on in this world where opinions are so artificial compared to the bible truth.

The bible truth is the real deal about everything that is going on in this world where phenomena are so artificial compared to the bible truth.

The bible truth is the real deal about everything that is going on in this world where spiritualism is so artificial compared to the bible truth.

The bible truth is the real deal about everything that is going on in this world where luck is so artificial compared to the bible truth.

The bible truth is the real deal about everything that is going on in this world where magic is so artificial compared to the bible truth.

The bible truth is the real deal about everything that is going on in this world where wishes are so artificial compared to the bible truth.

The bible truth is the real deal about everything that is going on in this world where lies are so artificial compared to the bible truth.

The bible truth hovers over this world every day like the sky hovers over the world.

The bible truth hovers over the heavens because Jesus Christ is the bible truth that is eternal in heaven above this world that will one day pass away with every artificial thing.

No One Can be More

No one can be more humorous than the Lord.

No one can be more wise than the Lord.

No one can be more superior than the Lord.

No one can be more loving than the Lord.

No one can be more great than the Lord.

No one can be more giving than the Lord.

No one can be more strong than the Lord.

No one can be more kind than the Lord.

No one can be more compassionate than the Lord.

No one can be more temperate than the Lord.

No one can be more fair than the Lord.

No one can be more beautiful than the Lord.

No one can be more knowledgeable than the Lord.

No one can be more discerning than the Lord.

No one can be more powerful than the Lord.

No one can be more faithful than the Lord.

No one can be more real than the Lord.

No one can be truer than the Lord.

No one can be more bold than the Lord.

No one can be more encouraging than the Lord.

No one can be more motivating than the Lord.

No one can be more trusting than the Lord.

No one can be more free than the Lord.

No one can be more gentle than the Lord.

No one can be more humble than the Lord.

No one can be more vibrant than the Lord.

No one can be more peaceful than the Lord.

No one can be more genius than the Lord.

No one can be more understanding than the Lord.

No one can be more intelligent than the Lord.

No one can be more cheerful than the Lord.

No one can be more skillful than the Lord.

No one can be more talented than the Lord.

No one can be more miraculous than the Lord.

No one can be more rich than the Lord.

No one can be more socializing than the Lord.

No one can be more clear than the Lord.

No one can be more precise than the Lord.

No one can be more visual than the Lord.

No one can be more stable than the Lord.

No one can be more glorious than the Lord.

No one can be more worthy than the Lord.

No one can be more patient than the Lord.

No one can be more convincing than the Lord.

No one can be more merciful than the Lord.

No one can be more forgiving than the Lord.

No one can be more holy than the Lord.

No one can be more direct than the Lord.

No one can be more sincere than the Lord.

No one can be more righteous than the Lord.

No one can be more creative than the Lord.

No one can be more present than the Lord.

No one can be more historic than the Lord.

No one can be more prophetic than the Lord.

No one can be more outgoing than the lord.

No one can be more healing than the Lord.

No one can be more in control than the Lord.

No one can be more energetic than the Lord.

No one can be more successful than the lord.

No one can be more relational than the Lord.

No one can be more on time than the lord.

No one can be more victorious than the Lord.

No one can be more active than the Lord.

No one can be more correct than the Lord.

No one can be more united than the Lord.

No one can be more brilliant than the Lord.

No one can be more captivating than the Lord.

No one can be more moving than the Lord.

No one can be better than the Lord.

No one can be more profound than the Lord.

No one can be more mysterious than the Lord.

No one can be more supernatural than the Lord.

No one can be more down to earth than the Lord.

No one can be more plain than the Lord.

No one can be more up to date than the Lord.

No one can be more spiritual than the Lord.

No one can be more alive than the Lord.

No one can be more communicating than the Lord.

No one can be more alert than the Lord.

No one can be more listening than the Lord.

No one can be closer to you and me than the Lord, if we love Him and keep His Commandments.

Is Heaven on Earth to Me

Believing in Jesus Christ is heaven on earth to me.

Loving Jesus and keeping His Commandments is heaven on earth to me.

My hope in Jesus is heaven on earth to me.

My trust in Jesus is heaven on earth to me.

My faith in Jesus is heaven on earth to me.

My testimonies about what Jesus brought me through is heaven on earth to me.

Jesus giving me the strength to go through my trials is heaven on earth to me.

Jesus answering my prayers is heaven on earth to me.

Working for Jesus is heaven on earth to me.

Jesus supplying all of my needs is heaven on earth to me.

Being a witness of Jesus is heaven on earth to me.

Reading the bible to know more and more about Jesus is heaven on earth to me.

Going to church to worship Jesus Christ is heaven on earth to me.

Living right unto Jesus is heaven on earth to me.

Giving Jesus the glory and praise is heaven on earth to me.

Spreading the good news about Jesus is heaven on earth to me.

Hearing sermons about Jesus is heaven on earth to me.

Participating in Sabbath school lessons about Jesus is heaven on earth to me.

Keeping Jesus first in my life is heaven on earth to me.

Praying to Jesus to bless others is heaven on earth to me.

Praying to Jesus to show mercy on others is heaven on earth to me.

Being thankful unto Jesus is heaven on earth to me.

Jesus protecting me from harm and danger is heaven on earth to me.

Jesus forgiving me of my sins is heaven on earth to me.

Jesus cleansing me from my sins is heaven on earth to me.

Being saved in Jesus Christ is heaven on earth to me.

Loving my neighbors like Jesus loves them is heaven on earth to me.

Not denying Jesus in the presence of my neighbors is heaven on earth to me.

Being content in Jesus is heaven on earth to me.

Waiting on Jesus to answer my prayers is heaven on earth to me.

Waiting on Jesus to work things out in my life is heaven on earth to me.

Talking to Jesus is heaven on earth to me.

Holding onto Jesus is heaven on earth to me.

Doing what Jesus tells me to do is heaven on earth to me.

Knowing that Jesus won't put on me more than what I can bear is heaven on earth to me.

Knowing that Jesus will not fail me is heaven on earth to me.

Knowing that Jesus will save me from my sins for confessing and repenting of my sins is heaven on earth to me.

Knowing that Jesus will never leave me or forsake me is heaven on earth to me.

Knowing that Jesus is coming back again one day soon to take me to heaven for being saved in Him is heaven on earth to me.

Many People Still Won't Give God the Glory and Praise

Many people still won't give God the glory and praise after seeing a solar eclipse that God created beyond this world.

Many people still won't give God the glory and praise after seeing a lunar eclipse that God created beyond this world.

Many people will give the glory and praise to the solar and lunar eclipse that is a creation of God.

Many people will get very excited about seeing the solar eclipse and lunar eclipse, but they will never get excited about a higher intelligence that created the heavens and earth.

Many people will see the solar and lunar eclipse and say that it is magical and be at a loss for words and emotional, saying it is amazing and a wonder, but God is above it all to be worthy of the glory and praise.

Many people still won't give God the glory and praise that God deserves above time that is like one second to an eternal and all-present God that a solar and lunar eclipse can't out-glorify and out-magnify.

Solar eclipses and lunar eclipses can only exist in the presence of time that is like a blink of an eye to an everlasting God who the path of totality can't ever measure up to and can't even glimpse God's eternality.

A Lot of People

A lot of people don't believe in Jesus Christ.

A lot of people believe in their talents.

A lot of people believe in their skills.

A lot of people believe in their job.

A lot of people don't believe in Jesus Christ.

A lot of people believe in their wealth.

A lot of people believe in their finances.

A lot of people believe in their theories.

A lot of people believe in their education.

A lot of people don't believe in Jesus Christ.

A lot of people believe in their plans.

A lot of people believe in their strength.

A lot of people believe in their health.

A lot of people don't believe in Jesus Christ.

A lot of people believe in their own words.

A lot of people believe in their feelings.

A lot of people believe in their heart.

A lot of people believe in their thoughts.

A lot of people don't believe in Jesus Christ.

A lot of people believe in their lies.

A lot of people believe in their greed.

A lot of people believe in their jealousy.

A lot of people believe in their grudges.

A lot of people don't believe in Jesus Christ.

A lot of people believe in their appetite.

A lot of people believe in their smarts.

A lot of people believe in their wickedness.

A lot of people believe in their pleasures.

A lot of people don't believe in Jesus Christ.

A lot of people believe in their desires.

A lot of people believe in their tricks.

A lot of people believe in their time.

A lot of people believe in their ways.

A lot of people don't believe in Jesus Christ.

A lot of people believe in themselves.

A lot of people believe in their eyesight.

A lot of people believe in their world.

A lot of people believe in their selfishness.

A lot of church folks don't believe in Jesus Christ.

A lot of church folks believe in their pride.

A lot of church folks believe in their gossip.

A lot of church folks believe in their favoritism.

A lot of church folks believe in their pretense.

A lot of church folks don't believe in Jesus Christ because they have no heart of true repentance to turn away from their sins that they hold onto.

A lot of people don't believe in Jesus Christ, who is the supreme belief over every other belief that will fail you and me for our souls to be lost.

Believing in Jesus Christ is supreme over only going through the motions of worship that will be a false worship unto the Lord, especially if church folks don't love one another like Jesus, who loves everybody inside and outside the church.

A lot of people don't believe in Jesus Christ, because many church folks denying Jesus before them in their changeable ways of not living by the bible that points us to Jesus.

We Just Don't

Sometimes when we think that we know people, we just don't.

Sometimes when we think that we know ourselves, we just don't.

We can fall short of not knowing something to be right or wrong.

Sometimes when we think that we know what to say, we just don't.

Sometimes when we think that we know what to do, we just don't.

We can fall short and not know people's true intentions.

Sometimes when we think that we know what to do, we just don't.

We can fall short and not know people's true motives.

We can fall short and not know people's true intentions.

We can fall short and not know our own true motives.

We can fall short and not know our own true intentions.

We can fall short and not know people's hearts.

We can fall short and not know our own hearts.

Sometimes when we think that we know someone, we just don't.

Sometimes when we think that we know what is good for someone, we just don't.

Sometimes when we think that we know what is good for ourselves, we just don't.

We won't be right all the time, no matter how much we know is right.

Sometimes when we think that we know Jesus, we just don't.

Jesus can speak to us in a way that we just don't know.

Jesus can do something in a way that we just don't know.

Sometimes when we think that we know Jesus Christ, we just don't know that Jesus can do something in a mysterious way.

There are Only Two Kinds of People

There are only two kinds of people in this world.

Righteous and wicked people live together each day since Adam and Even were cast out of the Garden of Eden.

They had children who grew up to have children of their own, which populated the earth with only two kinds of people.

The righteous and wicked have been living among one another for thousands of years.

The righteous are God's children and the wicked are the devil's human agents.

Every day there are only two kinds of people living in this world: the righteous who are saved in Jesus Christ and the wicked who are lost in their sins.

Just because someone is wicked, he or she doesn't have to remain that way.

He or she can choose to repent of their sins and turn to Jesus, who gives every person a chance to turn away from their wicked ways before it's too late.

There are only two kinds of people living in this world: the righteous and the wicked.

There are no other kinds of people in between those two.

Either you and I are on God's side or we are on the devil's side; there is no neutral ground to stand on day after day.

The righteous are all about living right by God's holy word that is forever right about Jesus Christ being the Son of God and the light of the world.

The wicked are all about doing their own will and not doing God's holy will from day to day.

You and I can choose to live a righteous life or choose to live a wicked life.

God doesn't force anyone to live right by Him.

God is a righteous God forever and ever, and only the righteous will enter into heaven when the righteous King of Glory comes back again to take His righteous children to heaven.

There are only two kinds of people existing in the world from day to day, and it's the right thing to love and obey Jesus while we live.

God is Not a God of Confusion

God is not a God of confusion because God will make things plain and simple for you and me.

When God tells us to do something, God will not confuse us in any way.

We can know that God is talking to us because it will make sense and not confuse you and me.

God is not a God of confusion because God will give us His Holy Spirit that will teach us all the truth that will not be confusing to us.

God has inspired men to write His holy word so it would not confuse anyone who the devil loves to confuse.

The devil has his human agents to misinterpret the bible scriptures and confuse people with by saying the truth is a lie.

God is not the author of confusion because God has His holy children who are filled with the Holy Spirit to interpret the bible scriptures the correct way so they don't confuse anyone.

It's the devil who is all about confusing people with the truth of God's holy word.

God made it so plain and simple for Adam and Eve to not eat the fruit from the tree of knowledge, good and evil, but the devil came along and spoke through the serpent to confuse Eve about what God had said so simply to her.

God is not a God of confusion.

Adam and Eve found this out the hard way by disobeying God, who told them the truth plainly and simply that they would die for eating that forbidden fruit.

The Lord is so Merciful to Us

The Lord is so merciful to us who don't deserve His mercy.

We don't deserve the Lord's mercy, no matter what good deeds we do day after day.

The Lord's mercy is so miraculous that we don't see it coming our way.

The Lord's mercy is very sure to let us know that we don't have control over the unknown that comes our way.

The Lord's mercy is our strong foundation that holds us up against the uncertain pits that the Lord's mercy keeps us from falling into.

The Lord is so merciful to us, even after we sin against Him and deserve to die in our sins.

The Lord's mercy is unfailing in protecting us, even when we can make excuses to the Lord for our wrongdoings.

The Lord's mercy is so powerful that it lets us know that we can't be in control of all our actions when one bad spur of the moment action can make us be so helpless.

The Lord's mercy protects us from being helpless in bad situations.

The Lord's mercy is supernatural in our sinful nature, which can cause us to be unaware of what bad is coming our way.

The Lord is so merciful to us every day that His mercy is like the wide-open sky that protects us while we enjoy the sunlight and moonlight and all the stars.

The Lord's mercy is a great thing that we don't deserve, no matter how many right things we do and all the right words we say.

The Lord's mercy is perfect beyond our imperfect lives that need His mercy upon our righteousness, which is like filthy rags before the Lord.